Romantic NORFOLK

JOHN DUCKETT

HALSGROVE

First published in Great Britain in 2008

British Library Cataloguing-in-Publication Data
A CIP record for this title is available from the British Library

ISBN 978 1 84114 814 4

HALSGROVE
Halsgrove House
Ryelands Industrial Estate
Bagley Road, Wellington,
Somerset TA21 9PZ
Tel: 01823 653777
Fax: 01823 216796
email: sales@halsgrove.com
website: www.halsgrove.com

Printed and bound by D'Auria Industrie Grafiche, Italy

ACKNOWLEDGEMENTS

As with my first book I wish to dedicate this book also to my darling wife Alison. Without her constant
patience, understanding and unwavering support this book would never have made it to print.

INTRODUCTION

Romantic Norfolk is a book containing a collection of fine art photographs taken by myself, Norfolk-born landscape photographer John Duckett. It mainly concentrates on inland Norfolk, including the Broads, as it is a companion to my previous book, *The Romantic Norfolk Coast*. However, it does still include some new coastal images as I feel that the Norfolk coast is just so amazing no book about the county could be complete without including at least a few them.

The photographs are not generally the normal bright and sunny record shots so often seen of the area, rather they are a selection of the fine art images that I sell as limited edition prints. They are intended to show a different, more romantic and dramatic side of Norfolk. I have tried hard to capture the timeless quality of the rural Norfolk landscape and avoid the hustle and bustle of the towns and villages. I have, therefore, deliberately concentrated more on the quiet lanes and rivers which criss-cross the county, capturing some images not often seen. That said there are, of course, aspects of Norfolk that no book would be complete without and, for that reason, poppies, churches and, of course, the Norfolk Broads are all featured in these pages, along with the aforementioned coast. As you would expect, whatever the subject, the county's amazing skies play a huge part in many of the shots you will see.

The book is a celebration of my two passions, these being the wild landscapes of Great Britain and landscape photography. Being Norfolk born and bred, I have always loved the many aspects and challenges that the landscape of 'Nelson's county' offers photographers, from the wide open arable fields, gently meandering rivers, ancient woodlands and the unique landscape of the Broads. The ancient peat diggings which created the Broads bring many visitors to the area, with nearly 200 miles of waterways, wind drainage pumps, reed beds and staithes to discover. This area attracts artists, naturalists and host a multitude of sailing boats, dinghies and motor cruisers of all shapes and sizes.

This selection of photographs shows the mood of these superb landscapes by capturing the atmosphere and colours of both the stormy dramatic days and cold still dawns of winter, and some of the beautiful evening light and sunsets of summer. Whether resident or visitor, the reader will get an insight into this remarkable county, whatever the season or weather.

In recent years with the threat of global warming and rising sea levels, the future of the Norfolk landscape, and particularly the Broads for which is it most famed, is in doubt. Existing sea defences will possibly be breached, flooding these low-lying areas with salt water, changing the ecology forever. Many homes and villages would have to be abandoned.

My interest in photography began back in my early teens whist on family holidays taken throughout the UK. My Mum, Joan, had always been a keen photographer herself, so Dad, Brian, and brother, Paul, were already quite used to spending much of their holiday waiting around for her to catch them up or stopping at every lay-by just in case there was a photograph to be had. This support and understanding really helped me in the earlier years and allowed me time to learn the importance of waiting for the right light conditions when taking landscape photographs. Years later I started a career as a sales representative in the building industry, covering the whole of Norfolk and some of Suffolk. Being on the road throughout the year and spending the majority of my time in more rural areas rekindled my love for seeing how the light can completely change the atmosphere of a landscape. Winters were best when the shorter days meant I was out and about to witness the amazing colourful skies of dawn and dusk. I often had my camera and tripod in the car boot nestled up against the brick samples and product catalogues. During this time the bleaker and stormier days had a bigger influence on me than the bright and sunny days. The shards of sunlight through stormy skies and diffused light seen on these days were what really excited me and made me determined to gain the skills to capture these scenes on the camera. To this day this influence is still clearly visible in my style of landscape photography. Career-wise it was all change and my work took me off the road and into the office. By this time, however, I was hooked on the great outdoors and with my wife, Alison, started to spend nearly all of my free time out in the countryside – hill walking in the Peak District and Lake District, holidaying in the Highlands and on the West Coast of Scotland, in the Yorkshire Moors and Dales, North Wales and Cornish coast – but the thing that really turned my early influences into what is now my passion for landscape photography was the many long winter walks on the bleak north Norfolk coast with Alison, to the extent that in recent years we have settled in north Norfolk within 15 minutes of the coast at Wells-next-the-Sea.

Over the years I have slowly developed my unique atmospheric style through experience and experimentation with different camera settings and filters. I spent many years using 35mm SLR film cameras using various colour and black and white print films as well as transparencies. Over this time I learned the techniques of metering, balancing exposure with filters, depth of field and composition as well as, of course, working with the light. Once I had learned the basics I used this experience to achieve what I believe to be my personal style. My landscapes have the emphasis on drama. Wherever possible I try to steer clear of the typical bright and sunny shots so often seen. I love capturing atmosphere in my images and spend hours waiting for the right light conditions and clouds. Bright sunshine and blue skies are not generally for me. I much prefer to produce a dramatic moody image. Four years ago I made the conversion from film to digital SLR cameras. It took a while to adapt to this new technology but I was determined to use my experience of film and still maintain the importance of getting it right in the camera and not relying on the computer afterwards.

It was not until quite recently that I started to turn my passion into a career. During 2004 I joined an on-line photography website and started to upload some of my images for the critique of others. On the whole my images went down really well and I started to realise that other people also liked my moodier take on landscape photography, not only my mum and Alison! From there I joined the Wymondham Photographic Society. It was there that I was encouraged to enter my images into their competitions and even a couple of small exhibitions. The images got a really good response and my confidence started to grow. After moving to north Norfolk it was just too far to travel to the club any longer and it was with regret that I had to leave. However, I will always be grateful for the confidence they gave me. In August 2005 I attended my first craft show at the Aylsham show in Norfolk. This was a great success and things started to take off. Now nearly four years later I have turned semi-professional and undertake over twenty shows and exhibitions per year selling limited edition photographic prints. I have work permanently for sale at galleries in Norfolk and also regularly sell prints throughout the country and overseas from my website www.jduckettimages.co.uk, as well as corporate images for use in advertising, publication in books and magazines, calendars and greetings cards.

An old wooden hut dwarfed by the surrounding autumn trees in Sheringham Park.

A fishing jetty, Blickling.

Evening light on a field of barley near the campsite at Stiffkey.

A rain storm approaches a field of golden barley on a summer's day near Flordon.

A leafy path through Smock Mill Common near Saxlingham Nethergate.

The new tower of Wymondham Abbey
viewed through a spring hedgerow.

The beech avenue in the late afternoon autumn light at Felbrigg.

Bulrushes at the edge of a frozen and snow-covered pond in South Norfolk.

A break in the clouds allows the sun to catch the winter trees in Blickling Park.

St Benet's Level mill reflected in the dyke. The long shutter speed gives a sense of movement in the reeds.

The warm morning light catches St Benet's Level mill before the storm arrives.

Autumn in Sheringham Park.

Window on the Broads – The red brick of St Benet's Level mill contrasts with the white wind pump at Thurne.

A shard of golden evening light shines through the storm clouds on to Blickling Hall.

Reflections – A still morning
on the Broads.

Golden morning on the River Thurne.

Boats moored in a quiet cutting on the Broads near Thurne.

Golden morning at Thurne.

A group of poppies at the edge of a barley field on a stormy day near Mundesley.

The Church of St Peter and St Paul at Salle seen over a field of golden wheat.

Swans on the River Wensum at Guist.

The winter sky reflected in the calm waters of the River Wensum at Guist.

A snowy road leads to Bintree Mill.

The angle of the snow-covered gate leads the eye to the trees beyond a pond in this winter scene near Bintree Mill.

A summer residence on the River Thurne at dawn.

A golden winter sunrise over the River Wensum at Guist. The light in the window of the cottage and the large tree give this a Christmas feel.

Sepia winter – A sepia effect has been added to this winter landscape near Little Snoring.

A single red poppy in a field of golden barley lit by the soft evening light.

One ear stands proud of the rest in a field of golden barley gently swaying in a summer evening breeze.

Forgotten bale in a field near Fulmodeston.

Starlings and flags in the rigging of the *Albatross* silhouetted against the dawn at Wells-next-the-Sea.

A tree silhouetted against a clear and crisp winter's dawn.

Frosty morning, Felbrigg.

The River Wensum at Guist on a snowy winter's dawn.

A windy winter's day at Brancaster Staithe.

The old sea defences at Happisburgh in the early morning light.

St Andrew's Church, Little Snoring – unusual because the tower is detached from the church.

A sunny but breezy February day at Turf Fen.

A cloud positions itself perfectly over this view of Turf Fen.

The River Wensum in flood near Guist.

The wind pump at Turf Fen.

St Benet's Level wind pump near Thurne reflected in the dyke.

A May Day storm clears over a field of oil seed rape near Stibbard, north Norfolk.

Evening light on a field of wheat at Fulmodeston, near Fakenham.

Wooden posts on Brancaster beach against the sunset.

A long shutter speed blurs the waves at Cromer on a grey morning.

Perfect reflections of boats moored under autumn trees at Barton Turf.

A still dawn over pleasure boats moored at Thurne.

St Benet's Level wind pump dominates the skyline near the River Thurne.

A perfectly still morning at a Broads retreat near Thurne.

Sheep grazing on a misty meadow near Thornage.

Poppy field, Wood Norton.

A wide open Norfolk sky reflected in the water of the River Thurne.

The derelict Brograve Mill viewed across the windswept reeds and dyke.

Boardman's, a skeleton mill on the River Ant near How Hill.

'Lovers Lane' in the shadow of St Benet's Level mill.

Colours of a Norfolk summer – Golden barley, blue sky and vivid red poppies.

A swamped boat on the marshes at Cley-next-the-Sea following a tidal surge.

A tree silhouetted against the dawn over Salhouse Broad.

A winter tree in the grounds of Binham Priory.

Evening light on Binham Priory.

Summer clouds reflected in the River Bure at Brampton near Aylsham.

The white wind pump at Thurne clearly reflected in the river at dawn.

Moorings at Barton Turf in the autumn late afternoon light.

A secluded waterway leading to Cockshoot Broad near Woodbastwick.

Looking through a stile leading to Brograve Mill.

Still moorings at Thurne.

A lone cruiser moored at Salhouse Broad at dawn.

A dyke covered in duckweed on Halvergate Marshes.

Dawn over the in-flood River Wensum at Ringland.

The thatched boathouse on the River Bure at Coltishall.

Rowing boats moored up for the evening on
Ormesby Little Broad.

Winter trees silhouetted against a magnificent sunset near Aylsham.

Returning after a day's fishing past the boat house at West Somerton.

Boats for hire at a jetty near the Eel's Foot Inn on Ormesby Little Broad.

Boat house and wind pump in the reeds at West Somerton.

Snowdrops in the woodland near Walsingham.

Snowy field at dawn near Swanton Novers.

A path beside the River Ant leading to Cleyrack Mill on a bright and breezy day near How Hill.

A single poppy in a field of barley on a stormy day near Wood Norton. The late afternoon light gives this image a romantic feel.

Old wooden posts in Ormesby Little Broad.

A boat moves swiftly past the banks of the River Bure near Horning.

Sprite at Martham Staithe.

The sunset beautifully reflected on a still Ranworth Broad.

Pleasure boats make their way past this spot on the River Bure at Horning.

Colourful rowing boats moored
at Martham Staithe.

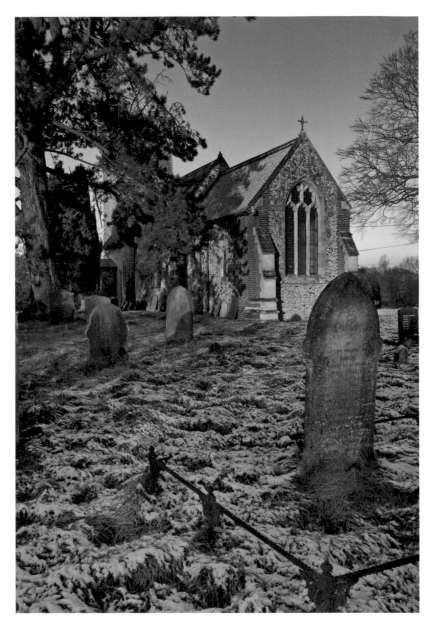

Evening light on St Edmund's Church, Swanton Novers.

Sunflowers and daisies – Sunflower crops are becoming more common in Norfolk.

Single poppy.

Dawn at Thurne.

A trio of boats covered for winter on the River Thurne.

Ducks resting in the last light on Ranworth Broad.

Frosty dawn near Swanton Morley.

Trees reflected in the smooth water of the River Wensum on a frosty morning near Swanton Morley.

Incoming wave at Horsey. A long shutter speed shows the movement of the wave over the pebbles.

A frosty dawn at Twyford.

Frost covered grasses on the bank of the River Wensum near Swanton Morley.

The old ruined flint walls of Castle Acre.

Looking up at the ruined walls of Castle Acre from the now grassy moat.

A unused gate and wooden fence leading into the lake at Felbrigg.

Golden reeds reflected in Felbrigg lake.

The River Nar as it flows past Castle Acre.

Spring at St Mary's and All Saints
Church, Newton.

Looking up at Castle Acre from the old moat.

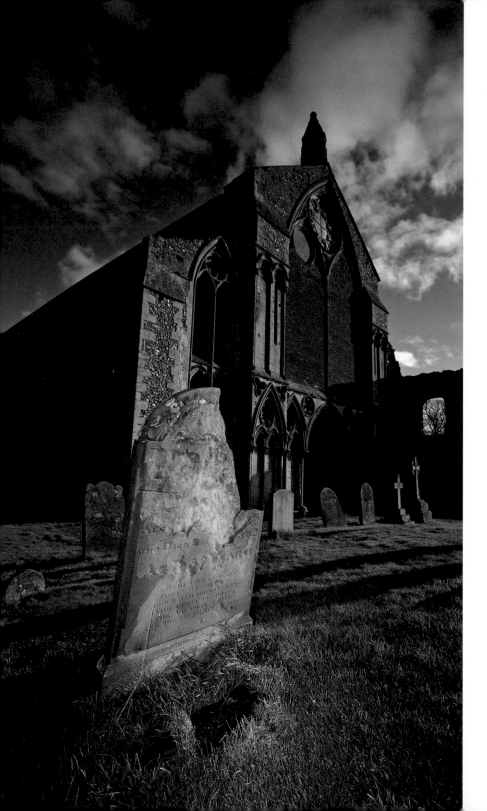

The light catches a broken gravestone
in front of Binham Priory.

The traditional red telephone box adds a splash of
colour on this snowy day in Stibbard.

Sunrise reflected in the River Bure at Lamas.

Buxton Watermill on the River Bure.
The use of a wide angle lens alters the
verticals of the mill giving it
a 'cartoon' feel.

Taken at dawn at Lamas, the River Bure has returned to its normal level after heavy rain but left its mark on the river bank.

A Norfolk flint wall at Felbrigg.

Mussel beds covered by the high tide at Brancaster Staithe on a stormy day.

One of the wind turbines in a field at Somerton spins against a stormy sky.

Snowy field at Blickling Park.

A lone tree in the snow in Blickling Park.

Palmer's Mill near Upton Dyke.

Snow-covered boats moored at Upton Dyke.

Last of the snow on the reed beds near Hickling Broad.

Kelling Heath in winter.

A boat resting in the mud near the reeds at low tide at Brancaster.

The view across the fields from Wiveton Downs near Blakeney in the evening light.

St Nicholas' Church, Potter Heigham.

A drainage dyke dissects the landscape near Potter Heigham.

Sunset reflected in the duck pond at Wood Dalling.

Houses beside the River Yare at Bawburgh.

The Church of St Andrew at Wood Dalling reflected in the village pond.

The clear waters of Whitlingham Great Broad.

The remains of wooden jetties on the River Yare at Bramerton.

A pleasure boat entering Rockland Broad from one of the cuts leading from the River Yare.

Reeds at the edge of Rockland Broad.

The top of Brograve Mill over the swaying reeds.

Sunlight on the water of Hardley Staithe.

Golden reeds, blue sky and white clouds at Hardley Staithe.

A spring day on Whitlingham Broad.

Looking across the field towards
St Benet's Abbey.

Contemporary sculptures beside Whitlingham Broad.

Sunrise over a frosty River Wensum near Swanton Morley.

A narrow wooden jetty at Coldham Hall pointing towards Brundall across the River Yare.

A field of oil seed rape under a stormy sky.

Strawberry fields near Little Snoring.

Fresh summer grasses in the breeze at Stiffkey.

The ford at Shotesham.

Storm clouds breaking up over a field of oil seed rape.

Rural view of sheep grazing in the meadow at Shotesham.

Barley field and gate in the early evening light near Blickling.

Rural view near the Roman camp, Caister St Edmund.

Hawthorn tree at Castle Acre.

Spring at Rockland Staithe.

A tidal creek at sunset near Morston.

A path through the bluebell woods at Blickling.

Bales in a field at harvest time.

The evening sky reflected in a pool of water on Stiffkey salt marshes.

Early dawn on the River Thurne.

Late afternoon light pours through a gate on the edge of a field of barley.

Golden reeds at the edge of Rockland Broad.

A modern sculpture near Coldham Hall
on the River Yare.

The snow covered trees reflected in Blickling lake.

A panoramic view of the dawn at Thurne.

A winter tree silhouetted against the sunset near Felbrigg.

Boats in blue – a boatyard at Hickling.

Stormy evening at Hickling Broad.

The beach on Hickling Broad.

'Welcome to Hickling'.

The wooden sea defences form a zigzag at Cart Gap.

An inquisitive local!

A wave rushes up the beach at Horsey.

Sunset over Cabbage Creek at Morston.

A field of barley near Marlingford in south Norfolk shimmers in the evening light.

A tree on the horizon draws the eye across the field of wheat.

A gap in the storm clouds allows the sun through to light Ellingham Sluice on the River Waveney.

The old derelict tower of Wymondham Abbey as seen from the churchyard.

A storm over the River Waveney which marks the Norfolk/Suffolk border near Geldeston.

Reflections in the fishing lakes on Broome Heath.

River traffic passes the swing bridge at Reedham.

A boat house on South Walsham Broad.